SEAL TEAM SIX

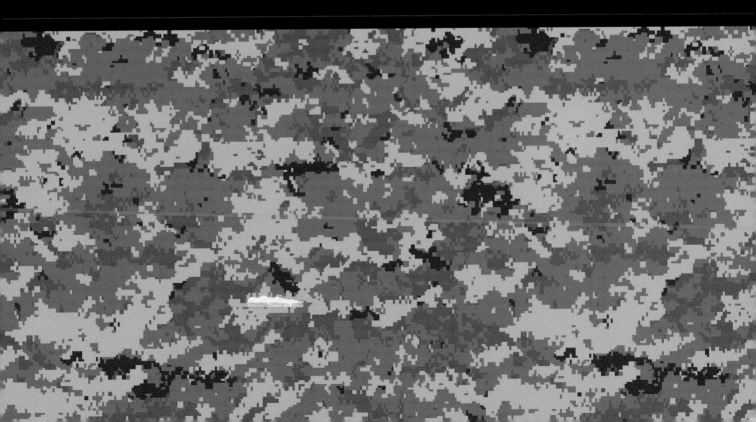

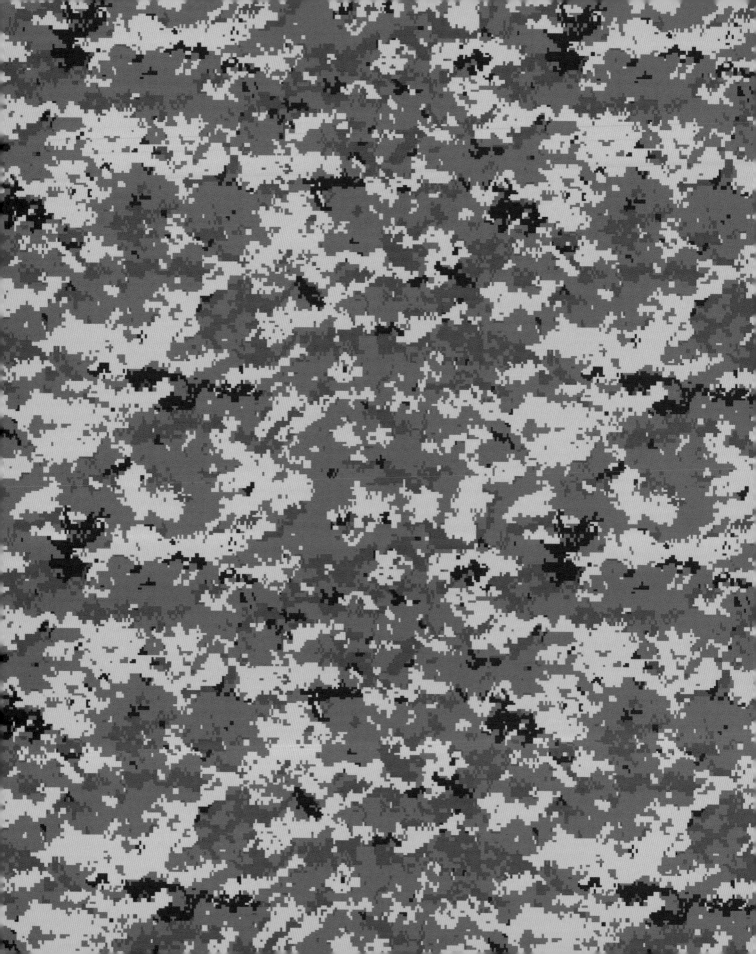

U.S. SPECIAL FORCES

SEAL TEAM SIX

JIM WHITING

CREATIVE EDUCATION · CREATIVE PAPERBACKS

PUBLISHED BY Creative Education and Creative Paperbacks

P.O. Box 227, Mankato, Minnesota 56002

Creative Education and Creative Paperbacks are imprints of

The Creative Company

www.thecreativecompany.us

DESIGN BY Christine Vanderbeek; **PRODUCTION BY** Liddy Walseth

ART DIRECTION BY Rita Marshall

PRINTED IN CHINA

PHOTOGRAPHS BY

Alamy (AF archive, Kathy deWitt, DOD Photo, Entertainment
Pictures, Moviestore collection Ltd, B. O'Kane, PJF Military
Collection, Stocktrek Images, Inc., US Marines Photo, US Navy Photo,
Oleg Zabielin), DVIDS (Petty Officer 2nd Class John Fischer, Petty
Officer 2nd Class Eddie Harrison, Cpl. Todd F. Michalek, Petty Officer
1st Class Michael Russell, Oscar Sosa, U.S. Navy/Petty Officer 3rd
Class Devin M. Monroe), iStockphoto (spxChrome), Shutterstock
(ALMAGAMI, gst, Carolina K. Smith MD)

LIBRARY OF CONGRESS CATALOGING-IN-PUBLICATION DATA

Names: Whiting, Jim, author.

Title: SEAL Team Six / Jim Whiting.

Series: U.S. Special Forces.

Includes bibliographical references and index.

Summary: A chronological account of the American military special
forces unit known as SEAL Team Six, including key details about
important figures, landmark missions, and controversies.

Identifiers: LCCN 2017051382 / ISBN 978-1-60818-986-1 (hardcover) /
ISBN 978-1-62832-613-0 (pbk) / ISBN 978-1-64000-087-2 (eBook)

Subjects: LCSH: 1. United States. Navy. SEALs—Juvenile literature.
2. United States. Navy—Commando troops—Biography—Juvenile
literature. 3. United States. Naval Special Warfare Development
Group—Juvenile literature.

Classification: LCC VG87.W542 2018 / DDC 359.9/84—dc23

CCSS:RI.5.1, 2, 3, 8; RH.6-8.4, 5, 6, 8

FIRST EDITION HC 9 8 7 6 5 4 3 2 1

FIRST EDITION PBK 9 8 7 6 5 4 3 2 1

U.S. SPECIAL FORCES

TABLE OF CONTENTS

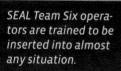

SEAL Team Six operators are trained to be inserted into almost any situation.

FORCE FACTS SEAL Team Six trained for a possible cruise ship hostage rescue operation during the 1992 Olympics in Barcelona, Spain. Fortunately, they did not have to put that training to use.

FORCE FACTS The SEALs who shot the *Maersk Alabama* hijackers arrived on-site after a 16-hour flight from Virginia. The flight included three midair refuelings.

INTRODUCTION

APRIL 8, 2009, BEGAN AS JUST ANOTHER DAY AT SEA FOR the American merchant ship *Maersk Alabama* and its captain, Richard Phillips. The ship was about 250 miles (400 km) off the coast of Somalia. Suddenly, four teenage pirates clambered onto the ship. It was the first time in nearly 200 years that pirates had boarded an American vessel. They planned on sailing it to Somalia and holding the ship and crew for ransom. The majority of the crew members barricaded themselves in a secure area of the ship. They shut down the ship's power to stop it from moving. So the pirates took Phillips into one of the ship's covered lifeboats as a hostage.

The following day, the destroyer USS *Bainbridge* arrived on the scene. It was the first of several United States Navy vessels that eventually surrounded the lifeboat. The pirates were unaware that several snipers from SEAL Team Six, an elite counterterrorism military unit, had flown from Virginia to the *Bainbridge*. On the destroyer, the SEALs took up positions facing the lifeboat.

One of the pirates boarded the *Bainbridge* to seek medical attention. The others began acting erratically. They appeared to be threatening Phillips with AK-47 assault rifles. Each SEAL aimed for a different pirate. The shots had to be precise headshots to prevent *involuntary muscle spasms* that could pull the triggers of the pirates' rifles. If that happened, bullets would spray the tight confines of the lifeboat. Increasing the difficulty, night had just fallen, and the lifeboat was bouncing up and down in the water. The SEALs fired simultaneously. All three shots slammed into their targets. Phillips was not hurt. The remaining pirate was taken to New York to stand trial.

Richard Phillips detailed his hostage experience in a book, which was made into the 2013 film Captain Phillips.

RISING FROM THE ASHES

SEAL TEAM SIX TRACES ITS ORIGINS BACK TO WORLD WAR II (1939–45). Armed only with knives, specially trained American scouts would swim to enemy-held beaches to conduct *reconnaissance* before invasions. Their missions expanded with the creation of Underwater Demolition Teams (UDTs), which served primarily in the Pacific. These teams blew up obstacles that might hinder invading forces as they came ashore. The UDTs continued their operations during the Korean War (1950–53). By then, there had been a rise in *unconventional warfare* around the world. The Army's Green Berets were established in 1952 to counter this threat. It was the country's first Special Forces unit.

In 1961, president John F. Kennedy ordered the formation of a naval Special Forces unit to complement the Green Berets. Because the unit would operate in a variety of environments—at SEa, in the Air, and on Land—its operators were called SEALs. The first two SEAL teams were formed on January 1, 1962. The men came to the unit from the UDTs. During U.S. involvement in the Vietnam War (1955–75), the SEALs performed hundreds of missions before the withdrawal of U.S. forces. Because of the green camouflage paint the men spread on their faces, the enemy called them "the men with the green faces." It likely was also a comparison to the Green Berets. Three SEALs won the Medal of Honor.

On November 4, 1979, hundreds of Iranians swarmed into the U.S. embassy in the country's capital city of Tehran. They

SEALs are often referred to as "frogmen" because of their training for and history of water-based operations.

FORCE FACTS Richard Marcinko served 15 months in prison for allegedly misusing government funds. After being released, he founded a security consulting firm and wrote his Rogue Warrior books.

captured several dozen Americans and held them hostage. The ordeal went on for months. Negotiations for the release of the hostages failed. President Jimmy Carter ordered a rescue mission code-named Operation Eagle Claw. Launched in April 1980, the operation was a spectacular failure. Eight American servicemen died. Footage of the smoldering wreckage of U.S. aircraft created worldwide embarrassment.

Military authorities analyzed the reasons for the mission's failure. They also started laying plans for a new counterterrorism strategy. Army Colonel Charles Beckwith had been one of the key planners for Operation Eagle Claw. His newly established and super-secret Delta Force would have carried out the rescue if things had gone according to plan. Delta Force specialized in land operations. Beckwith thought that the new strategy called for the addition of a *maritime* component to Delta Force. This component would help carry out operations such as rescuing hostages on cruise ships and attacking offshore oil rigs or coastal bases.

Lieutenant Commander Richard Marcinko had been one of the navy's representatives during the planning for Operation Eagle Claw. He served with SEAL Team Two in Vietnam and received four Bronze Stars. Marcinko agreed with Beckwith and quickly expanded the idea. Rather than devoting an elite new unit strictly to maritime missions, Marcinko envisioned it as an alternative to Delta Force. "So long as we carried water in our canteens," he said, "we'd be in a maritime environment—or close enough for me."

SEAL Team Six commonly works with the Night Stalkers, who fly them to target locations.

Marcinko's superiors endorsed the idea. It helped that several SEAL platoons had already undergone some counterterrorism training. Marcinko then came up with the unit's designation: SEAL Team Six. With the ongoing Cold War, he hoped to fool Soviet *intelligence* into believing that there were five other SEAL teams. In reality, there were still just the original two, plus the new unit.

Marcinko was ordered to get his unit operation-ready within six months. He began with 90 men—75 *enlisted* men and 15 officers. He encouraged what by navy standards was considered unacceptable grooming: long hair, beards, mustaches, and even earrings. This made the men seem like blue-collar civilians rather than highly trained operatives. Unlike the other two existing SEAL teams, SEAL Team Six's scope was worldwide. With just four hours' notice, they could *deploy* anywhere in the world. Despite the limited preparation time, Marcinko later said, "Even my enemies will admit that SEAL Team Six was the best-trained, deadliest, and most capable counterterror unit ever formed."

Marcinko was a brash man who developed a lot of enemies within the navy. He freely and even happily broke any rules he felt hindered his ability to structure SEAL Team Six the way he wanted it. Some of his critics claimed that loyalty to him was the main standard for admission to the unit. It does seem that he got rid of anyone who disagreed with him. One of the officers Marcinko dismissed during his years in command was William McRaven. Years later, McRaven

Before retiring in 2014, Admiral William McRaven held the title of "Bull Frog" as the longest-serving SEAL on active duty.

assumed command of all U.S. Special Forces. In 2011, he was one of the chief planners for Operation Neptune Spear. It was a highly publicized mission that resulted in the death of terrorist mastermind Osama bin Laden.

Despite his strenuous objections, Marcinko was forced to give up command of SEAL Team Six three years after founding it. Soon afterward, the unit saw its first action. It was a key element in Operation Urgent Fury—the 1983 invasion of the Caribbean island of Grenada.

In 1987, SEAL Team Six ceased to exist—on paper. The navy changed the unit's name to the Naval Special Warfare Development Group, or DEVGRU. (Unofficially, though, nearly everyone refers to it by the original name.) The reasons for the change are somewhat obscure. One opinion was that the navy wanted to distance the unit from Marcinko and emphasize its changing organizational structure. DEVGRU's stated mission is managing and testing current and emerging technologies that could be used by Naval Special Warfare units. In practice, it does a lot more, especially since the terrorist attacks of September

Before entering the training program, candidates must pass physical and psychological tests.

11, 2001. There has been a significant increase in both the number and the types of missions. According to a recent *New York Times* article, "Team Six has successfully carried out thousands of dangerous raids that military leaders credit with weakening militant networks."

Until recently, the navy credited those successes as accomplishments by SEALs in general, referring to the eight active SEAL teams in addition to SEAL Team Six. That served two purposes. One was attracting more applicants to the SEAL program. The high-risk, high-adventure missions that SEALs perform appeal to many young men who are thinking about joining the military. The other was helping to maintain the secrecy surrounding SEAL Team Six. However, that second condition changed with the successful attack on bin Laden. SEAL Team Six could no longer "hide in plain sight."

Another rare glimpse into the secret world of SEAL Team Six came on February 29, 2016. President Barack Obama awarded the Medal of Honor—the country's highest military decoration—to Senior Chief Special Warfare Operator Edward Byers in a ceremony at the White House. More than three years earlier, Byers and his fellow operatives had freed American physician Dilip Joseph from captivity at the hands of the Taliban, an Islamist fundamentalist militia that carries out numerous terrorist activities in Afghanistan. "Given the nature of Ed's service, there is a lot that we cannot say today," Obama said. "Many of the operational details of his mission remain classified. Many of his teammates cannot be mentioned." Byers undoubtedly spoke for many of his SEAL teammates when he said, "It's an affirmation of the job we do, an appreciation for the job we do. I'm going to continue being a SEAL and take whatever job or position is next for me."

Edward Byers is believed to be the first SEAL Team Six operator to receive the Medal of Honor.

FORCE FACTS SEAL Team Six squadrons have nicknames. For example, Red Squadron's nickname is "Indians," Blue Squadron's is "Pirates," and Gold Squadron is known as the "Knights."

JOINING THE BEST OF THE BEST

THE MEMBERS OF SEAL TEAM SIX BELIEVE THEY BELONG TO the best-trained, most effective special forces unit in the entire world. While most of its operations and structure remain highly classified, considerable information has been gleaned over time. The unit is based at Dam Neck Annex, just south of Virginia Beach, Virginia. To help protect their identities, the operatives normally wear civilian clothing when not on missions. A captain leads the unit, which is divided into color-coded squadrons. Four are assault squadrons: Blue, Gold, Red, and Silver. While sources vary, each squadron likely consists of 50 to 75 members and is headed by a commander.

In turn, the squadrons are divided into three troops, led by a lieutenant commander. Comprising each troop are several seven-man teams, led by a senior enlisted person. Black Squadron began as a sniper squadron. Following the 9/11 attacks, it transitioned to intelligence gathering. This unit has an estimated 100 members. Many of them are scattered throughout the world under deep cover in U.S. embassies or specially created *fronts* to perform their missions. In addition, up to 1,500 personnel provide a variety of administrative, logistical, intelligence analysis, and other functions. SEALs also frequently train with Delta Force. Sometimes, they carry out joint operations.

It's believed that SEAL Team Six has two dedicated squadrons of Sikorsky HH-60H Rescue Hawk helicopters to trans-

SEAL Team Six and Delta Force are among the most highly trained and secretive military forces.

port its operators. These choppers also provide fire support with Hellfire missiles and machine guns. In addition, the unit works closely with the Night Stalkers, the 160th Special Operations Aviation Regiment (Airborne). The Night Stalkers' MH-6 Little Bird helicopter can carry up to six SEALs and land in areas that are inaccessible to larger aircraft. The Night Stalkers also operate larger helicopters and have an exemplary reputation for delivering troops on time and on target.

The unit is rounded out by the Green Team, which is devoted to personnel selection and training. Members of the existing (and fully acknowledged) eight Navy SEAL teams can apply for SEAL Team Six. Becoming a SEAL in the first place is one of the most difficult processes in the entire U.S. military. The most famous part of training is Hell Week, a five-and-a-half-day period that pushes candidates to the limits of their physical and mental abilities. SEAL candidates undergo extreme sleep deprivation, hunger, and continuous discomfort during almost constant exercise. Much of that exercise immerses them in the chilly Pacific Ocean. An instructor notes that physical strength is only a small part of Hell Week. "Actually, it's 90 percent mental and 10 percent physical," he said. "(Students) just decide that they are too cold, too sandy, too sore, or too wet to go on. It's their minds that give up on them, not their bodies." Reportedly, only 30 percent of candidates make it through Hell Week. Many more months of arduous training await them before they finally become SEALs.

Those who want to move on to SEAL Team Six typically have at least five years of distinguished service and multiple deployments. The application process begins with intense *vetting*. Dozens of peers and commanders under whom the candidates served are asked for detailed evaluations. The best of the best proceed to a three-day screening interview. Those who pass are invited to join Green Team.

Green Team trainees are sometimes injured or develop hypothermia during the process.

Green Team is even more intense than SEAL training. The training lasts nine months and pushes trainees beyond their limits. "The point was not to meet the minimums, but crush them," said one man. "Success in Green Team was about managing stress and performing at your peak level—all the time." Another said, "A lot of people showed up at [training] who were much more physically capable than I was, football players and athletes in phenomenal shape, and they were the first to quit. Mental toughness is a must to make it through training, much less through combat."

To achieve that extreme level of toughness, each day begins with intense physical training: pushups, sit-ups, pull-ups, long runs, and other grueling activities such as pushing cars or even buses. Candidates may also average more than five parachute jumps per day during a month-long period. They run and swim at least five miles (8 km) daily and may lift weights for as many as four hours a day.

The object is to tire out the men before the "real training" that follows. This simulates the stress of real missions. Much of this training takes place in an expansive concrete structure that provides practice in close quarters combat (CQC). Movable panels can create a variety of scenarios, including hotels, houses, and shopping centers. As former SEAL Howard Wasdin notes, "I'm gonna put 50 pounds (22.7 kg) of equipment on you, give you 2 weapons and a sidearm, and we're going to go up and down stairs all day long, clearing different rooms. Some of them will be barricaded, some of them will have little kids in them, some of them will have people with machine guns shooting back at you." The men must make split-second decisions about whether to shoot. These decisions can

Trainees develop the mental toughness to focus and make correct decisions instantaneously.

mean the difference between life and death for the hostages they are seeking to rescue as well as for the men themselves. There's another source of stress: Every training exercise is closely monitored. The men know they are being observed by instructors with years of experience in virtually every conceivable situation. No error is too small to ignore. As a former SEAL notes, "You train and train, you go over things over and over, you do a ton of dry runs. When the door gets blown and you go in, you don't even think. It's just second nature, and you resort to muscle memory and your training."

Like Hell Week, Green Team dropout rates are substantial. The bottom line is that anyone joining the navy with the intention of becoming a member of SEAL Team Six has about a 1 in 150 chance of achieving that ambition. And to get there, he must first endure several years of intense physical and

During training, candidates move up from pistols to larger and more powerful weapons, such as M4s.

mental stress. Those who pass Green Team are ranked by the instructors. Then the men undergo a process that resembles a professional sports draft. The four assault squadrons take turns picking new members, based in part on the particular skills they are seeking. Once the men join their squadron, they are placed in one of three categories: deployed, training (at Dam Neck to further hone their skills and maintain their almost superhuman levels of fitness), or standby (ready at a moment's notice to deploy in response to a new situation).

Both while training and conducting their missions, the men rely on a variety of weapons. Many choose the Heckler & Koch MP7A1 submachine gun. Reportedly developed expressly for SEAL Team Six, this weapon's effective range is more than 200 yards (183 m). With the stock retracted, it is only 16 inches (40.6 cm) long. Its small size and lightness make it ideal for CQC. Mounting a suppressor on the front reduces the recoil to a bare minimum. This allows greater accuracy and a more rapid rate of fire. Another favorite is the M4A1 carbine, commonly used by a variety of Special Forces operatives. It can accommodate an array of accessories, including night-vision sights, a *foregrip*, and a grenade launcher. There are also several pistols. The six-inch (15.2 cm) Sig Sauer P239 is ideal for operators conducting *covert* intelligence, as it is easily concealed under civilian clothing. Snipers also have several choices. For especially long shots, the McMillan TAC-338—with an effective range of more than a mile (1.6 km)—is often the preferred choice.

Because of the thoroughness and length of the evaluation and training process, the team has a considerable number of men in their 30s. Reportedly, several of the men in Operation Neptune Spear were over the age of 40. As author Chris Martin observes, "The unit exists as something of an all-star collection of the most talented and experienced operators the [SEAL] community has to offer."

Operators regularly work on honing their skills wherever they are stationed.

FORCE FACTS The first season of the TV drama *Six* dealt with a mission to eliminate a Taliban leader in Afghanistan, which becomes complicated when it is revealed that an American citizen is working with the Taliban.

SEAL TEAM SIX IN THE MEDIA

U.S. SPECIAL FORCES

Despite a few high-profile missions, SEAL Team Six has remained shrouded in secrecy for almost its entire existence. Nevertheless, the unit is the subject of numerous books, films, and video games. Among many authors who have written about the group, three stand out: Richard Marcinko, Howard Wasdin, and Don Mann. All three were former members of SEAL Team Six. Each published an account of his experiences, and then called upon those experiences to write a series of adventure novels.

Marcinko wrote *Rogue Warrior* in 1992. It describes his experiences in Vietnam and founding SEAL Team Six. Two years later, he turned to fiction in *Rogue Warrior II: Red Cell.* Nearly 20 Rogue Warrior novels have followed. In an unusual twist, Richard Marcinko—a fictionalized version of the author—is the lead character. All the novels mix fact and fiction. They are characterized by continuous action and rough-edged humor with plenty of swearing. The series has attracted legions of fans and positive comments from critics. "The real nitty-gritty, bloody and authentic," is a typical comment.

Wasdin's *SEAL Team Six: Memoirs of an Elite Navy SEAL Sniper* benefited from perfect timing. It appeared on bookshelves in 2011, a week after the killing of Osama bin Laden. According to the *New York Times,* "Mr. Wasdin's narrative is visceral and as action-packed as a Tom Clancy thriller." A year later, Wasdin adapted it for teenage readers and called it *I Am a SEAL Team Six Warrior: Memoirs of an American Soldier.* "This is a great book for teens in-

Fast-roping allows operators to land in places where a helicopter cannot touch down.

FORCE FACTS Don Mann is known as the "high-mileage" SEAL. He's run about 75,000 miles (120,700 km) and biked another approximately 300,000 miles (482,800 km).

terested in joining the military, adventure fans looking for something meatier, and guys in general," reviewed *School Library Journal*. Wasdin has also written two novels: *SEAL Team Six Outcasts* (2012) and *SEAL Team Six Outcasts: Easy Day for the Dead* (2013).

Mann wrote *Inside SEAL Team Six: My Life and Missions with America's Elite Warriors* in 2011. Then he began his fictional series, featuring Chief Warrant Officer Thomas Crocker. First was *SEAL Team Six: Hunt the Wolf*, published in 2012. Mann stays abreast of current events in the series. In the fifth book, *SEAL Team Six: Hunt the Fox* (2015), Crocker and his team deal with a plot by the notorious terrorist group ISIS. The next book, *SEAL Team Six: Hunt the Dragon* (2016), focuses on the nuclear ambitions of North Korea. "A riveting and accurate description of how special operations units actually conduct counterterrorist operations in the field," said former CIA supervisor James Blount about *Dragon*. "If you are interested in reading a suspenseful, action-filled novel written by the 'real deal' instead of some amateur wannabe, pick up this book, or any of those in the 'SEAL Team Six' series." Mann turned his hand to practical matters in 2014, with *How to Become a Navy SEAL*. The book deals not only with the physical and mental requirements of joining the SEALs but also with the bureaucratic elements that recruits are likely to encounter. He expanded his horizons even further in 2017 with *Navy SEALs: The Combat History of the Deadliest Warriors on the Planet*.

Another first-person account about SEAL Team Six came from captain Richard Phillips. He published *A Captain's Duty: Somali Pirates, Navy SEALs, and Dangerous Days at Sea* in 2010. He included an interesting detail: the *Bainbridge* had sent over a change of clothing, which included a bright yellow shirt. He later realized it would help distinguish him from his captors. It proved unnecessary. He slid down in exhaustion at the moment the three Somalis leaped to their feet. "All of a sudden, shots rang out," he wrote. "Bangbangbangbangbangbang." His ordeal was over.

SEAL Team, a television series starring David Boreanaz that premiered in 2017, follows a subunit of DEVGRU.

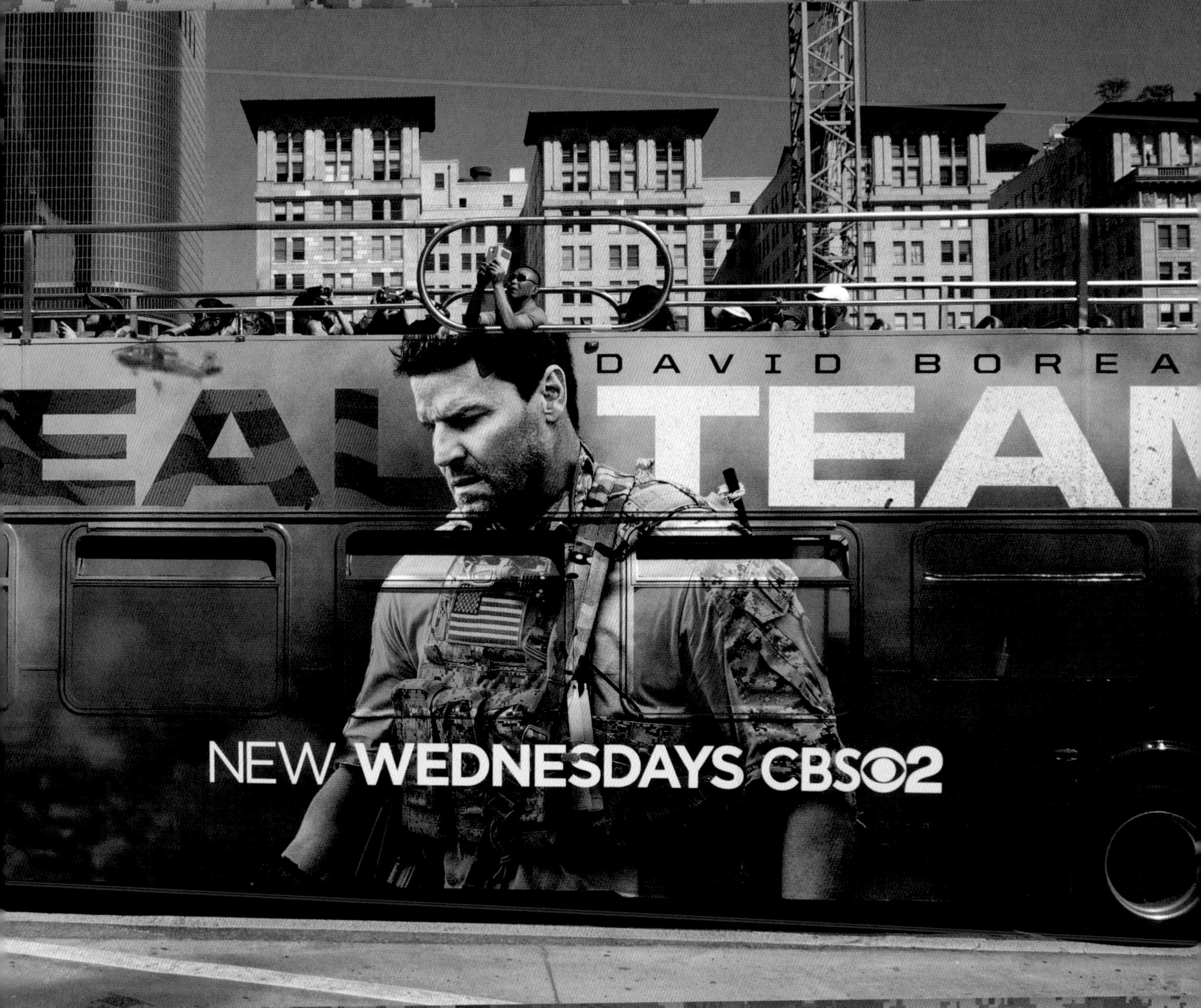
DAVID BOREA
NEW WEDNESDAYS CBS2

FORCE FACTS An entire 15-man troop of Gold Squadron died on August 6, 2011, when their helicopter was shot down in Afghanistan. It is the largest, single-event loss of life suffered by SEAL Team Six.

Not surprisingly, a number of books have been written about the bin Laden mission. Some of the more notable include *Manhunt: The Ten-Year Search for Bin Laden from 9/11 to Abbottabad* (2012) by Peter Bergen, a respected journalist and national security analyst for CNN. "Bergen has accomplished a journalistic feat: He manages to make the story of bin Laden's end sound new," wrote the *Washington Post*. "He has put together a real-life thriller that will be a must-read for years to come." Mark Bowden, noted for *Black Hawk Down*, his book about the ill-fated Special Forces raid in Somalia in 1993, wrote *The Finish: The Killing of Osama bin Laden* in 2012. "*The Finish* leverages access to key White House, military, intelligence, and foreign-policy officials—including President Obama himself— to get behind the intricate story of how SEAL Team Six was sent to Abbottabad, Pakistan, to kill Osama bin Laden," wrote *The Atlantic*. Chuck Pfarrer's *SEAL Target Geronimo: The Inside Story of the Mission to Kill Osama bin Laden* was released in 2011. *Kirkus Reviews*, which gave the book a starred review, described it as "catnip for readers who enjoy special-ops tales."

While receiving considerable reader and critical praise, another book also generated a different reaction. *No Easy Day: The Firsthand Account of the Mission That Killed Osama bin Laden* was written by "Mark Owen," a *pseudonym* for one of the SEALs who took part in the raid. Owen was later revealed to be Matt Bissonnette. Bissonnette hadn't received advanced clearance from the Department of Defense before publishing the book. The government forced him to forfeit nearly $7 million in earnings. The controversy expanded when evidence emerged that Bissonnette had talked some SEALs into serving as consultants for the video game *Medal of Honor: Warfighter* (2012) without getting official permission. The Defense department was especially concerned that classified information such as tactics, techniques, and procedures (TTPs) may have been included in the game. "I guess if you stretch it there, you could say that if [terrorists] played that video game enough based on real Navy SEALs' knowledge, [they] could

As shown in Black Hawk Down, DEVGRU and other forces worked together in the failed Battle of Mogadishu.

learn to counter some of those TTPs," said former assistant director of national intelligence John Miller. The makers may not have gotten their money's worth. The game received generally low ratings.

At least two fictionalized versions of the raid also exist. One is the graphic novel *Code Word: Geronimo*, by retired Marine captain and military film consultant Dale Dye and Julia Dye. The novel was released a mere four months after the raid. The other is *Osama's Angel* (2015), by Michael McWilliams. It takes the approach that bin Laden was captured rather than killed and undergoes interrogation. Many readers praise its military authenticity.

Two films are based on the operation. *Zero Dark Thirty* (2012) focuses on the painstaking intelligence work that eventually located bin Laden. It received five Oscar nominations, including one for best picture. Film critic Manohla Dargis from the *New York Times* noted that the movie "ends with the harrowing siege of bin Laden's hideaway by the Navy SEALs (played by, among others, Joel Edgerton and Chris Pratt), much of it shot to approximate the queasy, weirdly unreal green of night-vision goggles. Ms. [Kathryn] Bigelow's direction here is unexpectedly stunning, at once bold and intimate."

SEAL Team Six: The Raid on Osama bin Laden was released as a TV movie a few weeks before *Zero Dark Thirty*. Focusing on the raid itself, it was nominated for two primetime Emmy awards. TV viewers also tuned in to the History Channel's *Six*, which debuted in January 2017. It was renewed for a second season soon afterward. The series deals with the field operations of the SEALs and their daily lives. Ken Tucker of Yahoo TV said, "It's the brutal aspect of Rip [the lead character, played by Walton Goggins] that makes him a compelling figure to build a TV series around, mostly because so many dramas constructed around our military tend to **soft-pedal** the **morally gray**, or downright immoral, stuff."

The 2014 movie *The Interview* provides a change of pace from serious drama about the unit. In this political satire/spy comedy, North Korean dictator Kim Jong-un grants an interview to an American journalist. Things go wrong, and three SEAL Team Six operators have to rescue him.

Zero Dark Thirty covers the decade-long hunt for bin Laden and his death at the hands of the elite SEAL unit.

FORCE FACTS SEAL Team Six sometimes utilizes .50-caliber ammunition, which is powerful enough to penetrate automobile engine blocks.

SEAL Team Six has been involved in operations around the world.

FAMOUS MISSIONS OF SEAL TEAM SIX

U.S. SPECIAL FORCES

SEAL TEAM SIX DIDN'T HAVE TO WAIT LONG TO SEE ACTION after its founding. In 1983, a communist-backed group seized control of Grenada. With Cold War tensions still high, the U.S. feared that the new government could try to increase communist influence in the region. In addition, hundreds of American medical students were on the island. They could be held hostage. No one wanted a repeat of the Iranian hostage crisis. Planners quickly devised Operation Urgent Fury. "Urgent" meant that planning had to be not only secret but also swift.

Part of the plan went wrong right away. A group of SEALs was supposed to perform a daytime parachute drop into the ocean with two boats. They would pick up U.S. Air Force personnel from nearby ships and bring them ashore to mark a parachute drop zone for incoming Army Rangers. The planes were delayed. The SEALs had to parachute into a stormy ocean after nightfall. Four men, each laden with more than 100 pounds (45 kg) of gear, disappeared. So did one of the boats. The other SEALs, packed into the remaining boat, were swept out to sea. Fortunately, they were rescued.

The primary SEAL mission involved rescuing governor-general Paul Scoon, who had been placed under house arrest. This plan also went awry. The operation called for helicopters to drop about 25 SEALs into the compound where Scoon was being held. They would release him, then board the helicopters and fly to safety. But heavy ground fire drove off one helicopter. So only half the men got out. They didn't even have a radio. For several hours, the badly outnumbered SEALs fought off waves of attackers. Then

FORCE FACTS Cairo, the dog on Operation Neptune Spear, was a Belgian Malinois. His job was to sniff out any bombs and help keep curious neighbors away.

three armored personnel carriers began moving into position against them. Fortunately, the SEALs found a working landline. They used it to call in close air support, which eliminated the immediate threat and continued to cover them throughout the rest of the day and all night. A detachment of Marines fought its way to the compound the following morning and performed the *extraction*. By the time it was over, the SEALs had inflicted dozens of *casualties* without suffering any losses themselves.

In 2009, intelligence operatives located Saleh Ali Saleh Nabhan, a high-ranking *al Qaeda* leader whom they had been hunting for several years. He was responsible for several terrorist attacks in Africa. He was also active in recruiting potential al Qaeda members to help overthrow the weak Somali government. Military officials decided to use SEAL Team Six. They also decided to attack in daylight to make sure the target was indeed Nabhan. "Let's do it very quickly, very swiftly and confirm he's gone," said one official. Several Night Stalker Little Bird helicopters and SEALs attacked the two trucks carrying Nabhan and other terrorists on a remote road in Somalia. The fight ended quickly. All the terrorists were killed. No SEALs were hurt. The SEALs took away the bodies as well as computers and other intelligence information.

Two years later, SEAL Team Six's Red Squadron undertook what is probably the most famous Special Forces mission ever. Operation Neptune Spear was designed to take down terrorist mastermind Osama bin Laden. He had seemingly vanished nearly 10 years earlier. But painstaking work by U.S. intelligence agencies finally discovered what was believed to be his hiding place. It was in Pakistan. After months of further investigations, President Obama gave the "go" order. He did not notify the Pakistani government. Twenty-three members of SEAL Team Six—along with a translator and a highly trained dog named Cairo—crowded into two Night Stalker MH-60 Black Hawk helicopters under conditions of the greatest secrecy at their base in Afghanistan. Two Chinook

Because joining the unit requires years of experience, most operators are in their 30s or older.

helicopters carrying more SEALs waited just inside the Pakistani border to provide reinforcements. Several Air Force jets were on standby in case the Pakistanis detected the Black Hawks and tried to cut them off.

After a ground-hugging 90-minute flight, the Black Hawks arrived on target undetected. But one of the pilots began losing control in unusual atmospheric conditions as the helicopter hovered above the compound. He deliberately crashed the aircraft—a "soft landing"—in which no one was seriously hurt. The SEALs shot their way into the house, killing several people without suffering any casualties. They rushed upstairs, where they came face-to-face with bin Laden. Two bullets—one in the chest and the other just above his left eye—ended his life. With President Obama and key members of his national security team waiting anxiously, a SEAL radioed, "For God and Country, Geronimo [a code word meaning they had located bin Laden], Geronimo, Geronimo, Geronimo, EKIA [enemy killed in action]." Then the SEALs scoured the house. They gathered all the computers and other intelligence they could find.

Carrying bin Laden's body, they boarded the surviving Black Hawk and a Chinook that flew to the compound to replace the downed Black Hawk. Both helicopters returned to the base in Afghanistan.

To the country as a whole, it was a monumental achievement. The *New York Daily News* summed up the country's feelings by running a picture of bin Laden on the front page next to a huge headline that read, "Rot in Hell." Many people remember what they were doing when they heard the news. Bin Laden had hoped to go out in a blaze of glory. The SEALs made sure that didn't happen. Instead, as journalist Peter Bergen noted, "Bin Laden died surrounded by his wives in a *squalid* suburban

SEAL Team Six entered the spotlight after the success of Operation Neptune Spear.

compound awash in broken glass and scattered children's toys and medicine bottles—testament to the ferocity of the SEALs' assault on his final hiding place."

Five months later, American aid worker Jessica Buchanan and her Danish colleague Poul Thisted were in Somalia on a humanitarian mission. They were teaching people how to avoid the thousands of land mines sprinkled throughout the country. Somali bandits brandishing AK-47 assault rifles kidnapped them. Buchanan was sure she and Thisted would be killed. Instead, the bandits held them for ransom. As negotiations dragged on during the next three months, hunger was their constant companion. Each day, their captors gave them only a can of tuna and some bread. They slept outside, sometimes in torrential downpours. They had to deal

After bin Laden's death, Pakistan's government demolished his Abbottabad compound.

with the ever-present anxiety that their captors might get tired of waiting and kill them. Sometimes the Somalis would point guns at them or hold knives to their throats. On top of everything else, Buchanan developed a serious and painful infection.

One night in late January, Buchanan heard gunshots. A pair of hands roughly grabbed her. She thought she was about to die. Then a voice said, "Jessica, we're with the American military. We're here to take you home, and you're safe."

American officials involved in negotiations had learned of Buchanan's worsening physical condition. They decided on a rescue operation. About two dozen members of SEAL Team Six parachuted into Somalia. They landed about two miles (3.2 km) from the compound where Buchanan and Thisted were being held. As they proceeded toward the site, they came under fire. They shot back, killing the guards without suffering any casualties. Then the SEALs whisked the two hostages to safety. "I don't know that there is (another) nation that could pull this thing off with the speed, precision, and stealth that these forces did," said a senior defense official. "It is a reflection of the kinds of counterterrorism skills that we have nearly perfected over the last decade of war." As the helicopter carrying Buchanan lifted off, a SEAL gave her a small American flag. "I just started to cry," she said. "At that point in time I have never in my life been so proud and so very happy to be an American."

To SEAL Team Six, the rescue was an ordinary day at work. Admiral McRaven summed up the men's feelings by saying, "It is what we do. We get on helicopters, we go to objectives, we secure the objectives, we get back on helicopters, and we come home." The War on Terror will likely continue long into the future. As a result, SEAL Team Six will be getting on many more helicopters, securing objectives, and returning home for years to come.

When not deployed, operators remain in top form by testing their field readiness.

FORCE FACTS In 2002, SEAL Team Six members protected Afghan president Hamid Karzai during an assassination attempt.

Although the unit specializes in maritime missions, its operations have expanded to many settings.

FORCE FACTS When Richard Marcinko formed SEAL Team Six, he said his men were better shooters than Delta Force. A group of SEALs backed up his words by defeating a Delta Force team in a shootout.

GLOSSARY

al Qaeda – a fundamentalist Islamic organization founded by Osama bin Laden

casualties – people injured or killed in an accident or a battle

covert – hidden, secret

deployed – moved personnel into position for military action

enlisted – describing those who sign up voluntarily or are drafted for military duty at a rank below an officer; they compose the largest part of military units

extraction – the safe withdrawal from a mission

foregrip – the handle of a weapon mounted under the front part of the barrel

fronts – fake organizations set up to conceal the purpose of their true activities

intelligence – information about movements and strength of forces of an enemy

involuntary muscle spasms – sudden, uncontrolled muscular movements

maritime – relating to the sea

morally gray – no absolute right or wrong; having both good and bad points

pseudonym – a fictitious name used by an author to conceal his or her true identity

reconnaissance – a search to gain information, usually conducted in secret

soft-pedal – to play down the more unpleasant parts of something

squalid – extremely dirty or filthy

unconventional warfare – warfare conducted behind enemy lines, usually by small groups of fighters using guerrilla tactics

vetting – carefully examining and analyzing

FORCE FACTS Although assault squadrons are male-only (as of 2018), Black Squadron includes women, in the belief that a man and a woman doing covert reconnaissance together are more likely to blend in with the surrounding population than a single man or group of men.

SELECTED BIBLIOGRAPHY

Buchanan, Jessica, and Eric Landemalm. *Impossible Odds: The Kidnapping of Jessica Buchanan and Her Dramatic Rescue by SEAL Team Six.* With Anthony Flacco. New York: Atria Books, 2013.

Couch, Dick, and William Doyle. *Navy SEALs: Their Untold Story.* New York: William Morrow, 2014.

Frederick, Jim. *Special Ops: The Hidden World of America's Toughest Warriors.* New York: Time Books, 2011.

Hamilton, William H. Jr., and Charles W. Sasser. *Night Fighter: An Insider's Story of Special Ops from Korea to SEAL Team Six.* New York: Arcade, 2016.

Marcinko, Richard, with John Weisman. *Rogue Warrior.* New York: Pocket Books, 1992.

Owen, Mark, with Kevin Maurer. *No Easy Day: The Autobiography of a Navy SEAL; the Firsthand Account of the Mission That Killed Osama bin Laden.* New York: Dutton, 2012.

Phillips, Richard, with Stephan Talty. *A Captain's Duty: Somali Pirates, Navy SEALs, and Dangerous Days at Sea.* New York: Hyperion, 2010.

Wasdin, Howard, and Stephen Templin. *SEAL Team Six: Memoirs of an Elite Navy SEAL Sniper.* New York: St. Martin's, 2011.

WEBSITES

Beyond Neptune Spear: The (Open) Secret History of SEAL Team Six

https://sofrep.com/11883/beyond-neptune-spear-the-open-secret-history-of-seal-team-six-part-1/

Read about the history and training of SEAL Team Six, with particular emphasis on its formation and recent events.

DEVGRU/SEAL Team Six

http://www.americanspecialops.com/devgru/

Find detailed information about SEAL Team Six, including organization, equipment, and photos.

READ MORE

Brush, Jim. *Special Forces.* Mankato, Minn.: Sea-to-Sea, 2012.

Cooper, Jason. *U.S. Special Operations.* Vero Beach, Fla.: Rourke, 2004.

INDEX